Thomas Meek

An Essay on the Liberty of the Press

In which the rational and prudential limits of the noble invention of

printing are properly defined

Thomas Meek

An Essay on the Liberty of the Press
In which the rational and prudential limits of the noble invention of printing are properly defined

ISBN/EAN: 9783337315610

Printed in Europe, USA, Canada, Australia, Japan

Cover: Foto ©ninafisch / pixelio.de

More available books at **www.hansebooks.com**

AN

ESSAY

ON THE

LIBERTY OF THE PRESS:

IN WHICH THE

RATIONAL AND PRUDENTIAL LIMITS

OF THE

NOBLE INVENTION

OF

PRINTING

ARE PROPERLY DEFINED.

⸻⸱⸱⸱⸱⸱⸱⸱⸻

Salus populi suprema lex.

⸻⸱⸱⸱⸱⸱⸱⸱⸻

BY THE REV. T. MEEK, A. M.

⸻⸱⸱⸱⸱⸱⸱⸱⸻

SOUTH SHIELDS:

PRINTED FOR THE AUTHOR,

At the Minerva Office,

BY W. HALLGARTH, JUN. THRIFT-STREET.

———

1799.

PREFACE.

THE subject of the following Essay is highly interesting at any time, but more especially at the present juncture. The period has now arrived when government has thought proper to interfere, and thus exert its parental authority over the conduct of its children. I do not flatter myself that the subsequent Essay will give universal satisfaction, because it is next to impossible to treat a political subject in such a manner as to give offence to none. I have, however, deduced my arguments from immutable and eternal principles, which will hold true though the whole world was reduced to nothing; so that the republican or the friend to monarchy, the whig or the torie, cannot view these pages as the effect of party spirit. I have only to add that if the man who publishes his sentiments to the world is afraid, or ashamed to avow them, they ought to be buried in everlasting oblivion. The debauched villain who vends his anonymous poison by means of the press, will now be obliged to come forward in his native deformity, or remain for ever behind the scene. Merit will now lift up its head in triumph, and general utility be the employment of the press. Before such a step can be proved to be tyrannical, it must first be shewn that government is not the political parent of a country, and that the happiness of the people should be none of its concerns. To assert this, however, would be madness and extravagance, and to endeavour to prove it, an herculean task. I meddle not with the motives which may have induced government to take such a step, but I flatter myself that it will ultimately be productive of the most beneficial effects. It will have a tendency to screen us from the displeasure of the Almighty, by suppressing such publications as have brought his curse upon us.

AN

ESSAY

ON THE

LIBERTY OF THE PRESS.

———⟨⟩———

OF all the arts which have contributed to
the improvement and civilization of mankind,
we may justly consider that of printing as one
of the most beneficial. How imperfect was
the knowledge of the human race, how circumscribed, how difficult in the acquisition,
and how easily forgotten, before the sublime,
the elegant, the commodious discovery of the
use of types! Oral tradition was superseded
by a clumsy carving on the bark of trees, on
waxen tables, and such like; and this rude
attempt to transmit science to posterity, was
followed by the tedious practice of writing

B

upon vellum. A load of parchment of some stones in weight, could not contain the useful, important information of a single volume in print. What a noble invention! We speak of the dark ages prior to its discovery; but God alone can tell what darkness would have been the fate of Europe before this time, had that inquisitive genius never been born, who was the highly honored instrument of our emancipation from ignorance. The nativity of great men, and the annual commemoration of wonderful events, have been superstitiously observed in every age of the world; but the birth-day of the soldier who complimented mankind with the art of printing, should never be forgotten.

It is not to be wondered at, if the gradual improvement of this art met with every suitable encouragement, till it arrived at its present perfection. Individuals and states would soon find their interest in bringing it to maturity, and monarchs could not consider it as beneath

their dignity to countenance it by premiums.
To feel and acknowledge the excellence of
the human faculties, and to be sensible of
the value of every thing subservient to their
cultivation, are the necessary consequences of
a moment's reflection. Man left to himself,
is only a very few removes from the brutes
that perish; but by the study of useful and
ornamental science he becomes truly dig-
nified, resembles his maker in many noble
endowments, and can advance in the love
and practice of those things which will be
eternally advantageous.

Since the invention of printing, the dif-
ficulty of purchasing and perusing authors has
been unspeakably diminished; every thing
valuable in ancient manuscripts has been con-
cisely imparted to the world, and many interesting productions entirely new, have con-
tinued to illuminate the minds of men. The
poor have the highest reason to remember the
discovery with gratitude, since it places the

means of moral, religious, and mechanical improvement within their reach. The Bible, which contains the concerns of an eternal world, and the method of securing the divine favor through everlasting ages, can be purchased at a very small expense by the lowest ranks in life.

It is the duty of every well regulated government to encourage all works of science, all moral and mechanical investigations, as tending either to explain and enforce our duty to God, society and ourselves, or to instruct the industrious tradesman how to perform his work with the least possible expense, and the greatest facility. All men are not equally possessed of eminent abilities, nor of the power of application to study and enquiry. The few who are thus endowed, and who are willing to devote a life of thirty or forty years to the service of their country, in improvements, experiments, or in making discoveries, ought to have all the encouragement which the state

can impart.* If they are timid, and too fond
of remaining in obscurity, they should be
diligently sought out, stimulated to come
forward, and animated with the hopes of
being esteemed, honored and rewarded. If
they are poor (and riches seldom belong to
men of understanding;) it becomes the public
to free them from embarrassment, by defray-
ing the expenses of those labours which may
prove the glory of humanity, the defence of
real religion and rational liberty, or the source
of inexpressible advantage to the merchant or
mechanic. Many valuable manuscripts have
been rescued from oblivion, if not utter destruction, by commendable research, which
would have been permitted to become the prey
of the moth, or devoted to the flames by un-
assuming merit. The greatness and glory,
or the fatal stupidity of any nation, may be

B 3

* Perhaps no period can be found in the history of England in
which more encouragement was ever given to men of investigation
and research, than during the reign of his present Britannic Majesty,

ascertained from the encouragement given, or
the contempt shewn to works of real genius,
utility and pleasure. When a Peter Pindar
receives *thirty shillings* a copy for his outrages
on decency, and his burlesques on common
sense, while genuine master pieces of a digni-
fied understanding can scarcely pay the printer,
—the Lord help our country, say I, for it
is arrived at dotage.

Having applauded the invention of printing,
not more highly than I am persuaded it deserves, I trust I shall be considered as sincere
at least, if I defend the necessity of circum-
scribing its present extent, however much a
large proportion of mankind may be disposed
to differ from me in opinion. · The liberty of
the press has so corrupted the taste of Britons,
and thrown it into such a dangerous putrid
fever, that I scarce know what antiputrescents
will remove the distemper. It has made us
incapable of discerning genuine merit, and
consequently unwilling to reward its possessor.

O Britain ! while the historic page shall transmit to posterity, that you suffered a *Chatter-
ton* to die in obscurity and want, the world
must stand astonished at your monstrous stupidity and horrid ingratitude. But could
men be restored to themselves by the everlasting exclusion of those works that level
them with the brutes, the golden age for merit
would instantly spring up. Then would some
acquire ease and independence by the exertions
of their genius, while such as now make a figure
in the world would be buried in oblivion.

Were I to assert, that government ought to
circumscribe the liberty of the press, thousands
would listen to me with the profoundest indif-
ference; such a step would be considered by
others as a master-piece of despotism, and
perhaps others might view it as highly meritorious. It ought, however, to be remem-
bered, that it could neither be censured nor
applauded, till its precise object should be
known and accurately defined. Perhaps there

is not a phrase in the English Language more vague and indeterminate in its signification than " the liberty of the press." Should that infamous publication of Thomas Paine's, called the Age of Reason, be prohibited, * on pain of incurring the penalties of a high misdemeanor, that would be a death blow at the press in the estimation of some. Were government to punish the printers and venders of Mr Burke's writings, a vast multitude would perhaps sigh and say, there goes the liberty of the press! In short, the opinions of mankind upon this subject are not less diversified than their faces, and therefore it becomes extremely difficult, as well as delicate, to descant upon it. In what I have to advance, I wish to stand clear of all party disputes; and since I shall deduce my arguments from immutable and eternal principles, I will be the more likely to reach conviction without giving offence. In this manner I will evade all controversy about the mischief which it is pretended has

* It was not prohibited when this Essay was begun.

always followed from such a step as the above. In some countries, it may be deemed a pitiful subterfuge of absolute monarchy, to keep men easy under their chains, and in this country it may be viewed by some as the forerunner of that euthanasia of the British Constitution predicted by Mr Hume. These opinions and disputes are nothing to me, and absolutely foreign to my present purpose.

My first immutable and eternal principle is this ;—that to restrain the exercise or operation of any thing which is calculated to increase the substantial knowledge, or to improve the morals of the human race, would be the most consummate tyranny and insufferable despotism. Men have indiscrimately a right to enjoy a free access to rational information, if calculated to promote their present happiness, their meetings for a better life, and to perpetuate the existence of social order. It is the incumbent duty of all good governments to watch over the morals of the subjects with a parental anxiety,

because the happiness of the body politic de-
pends on their cultivation. This has engaged
the attention of the wisest legislators since the
commencement of time, of which a Solon and
a Lycurgus might be selected as examples.
If a father has at any time reason to reflect on
his own criminal folly and inattention in neg-
lecting the moral improvement of his offspring,
and permitting their minds to resemble an
unweeded garden, or the vineyard of the slug-
gard; the same compunction, in similar cir-
cumstances, ought to be felt by the political
parent or guardian of every nation,—I mean
its government. Every family is a nation in
miniature, and therefore the analogy from the
one to the other is fair and conclusive.

Now, what kind of publications must all
men grant to be calculated to increase the *substantial knowledge*, and to improve the morals
of the human race? Surely they are such as
the works of *Newton, Ferguson, Halley, Keil,*
in the departments of natural philosophy and

astronomy; *Euclid, Simson, Bonnycastle, Playfaire,* in geometry; *Atterbury, Hervey, Tillotson, Connybeare, Leland, Hume, Robertson,* and such like, in divinity and history, with every instructive publication on manufactures, agriculture, and the fine arts. Here I cannot run the risk of giving just cause of offence, because there is not a man upon earth, if he is *compos mentis,* who can be so ridiculous as dispute what we have now asserted. No wise government will ever prohibit such publications as the above, because it must intuitively discover that the more extensively these are circulated, and the more perfectly they are understood, its hands are proportionably strengthened, and its stability insured. Ignorance and wickedness are the only enemies which an excellent constitution and a lenient administration can ever know. I distinguished above, between knowledge and substantial knowledge, because there are ten thousand things which a man may know, that are either beneath his dignity, or a disgrace to his nature.

The arts of legerdemain, boxing, and gaming, are the dismal relicts of gothic barbarity, and only fit for lunatics or children.

Upon the same principles ought all profane, licentious, and infidel publications to be prohibited, as the very permission of them is a breach of the most sacred trust that can be committed to any government. It was therefore a pleasing sight to behold in the public prints,—The King versus the Publisher of Paine's Age of Reason, and to see the stupendous talents of Mr Erskine employed in leveling it to the dust. This may be supposed to belong more emphatically to the sons of the church, because the inculcating of moral precepts is a clerical duty. We grant it is; but such is the depravity of the human heart, that if men can procure volumes of obscenity from the press, no denunciations from the pulpit will deter them from perusing them. And it is needless to repeat what has been in effect said already, that the genuine felicity of a nation is in proportion to the purity of its morals, or the rectitude of their conduct of whom it is composed. Excessive luxury and dissipation carry misery in their train. Their escutcheon is, damnation to good order, and they extinguish all those manly energies which make a nation happy. Thus we give a death-blow to all profane ballads, to licentious poetry of every kind, though it should come from the polluted. pen of a nobleman, and to all secret histories of female prostitution. I know there is not a man in the island who can prove, to the satisfaction of sound reason, that government ought not to interfere in this respect. It is its duty, it is its interest, and it would therefore be a sturdy assertion, that such restraints on the press could be the result of despotism. They would discover a spirit truly philanthropic, and a most ardent wish for the extension of human felicity. I have no hesitation in affirming, that the licentiousness of the press, called by some its liberty, has made more thieves, rogues, pick-pockets, rakes, and prostitutes than would people a continent. Witness, ye rapes, robberies, murders, trials, and condemnations without number, if I can possibly be mistaken. No ! corrupt nature is unquestionably chargeable with innate corruption, but the infernal publications formerly alluded to, and which it is equally as criminal to print as to tolerate, have taught men to be wicked by method and rule, to invent new modes of accumulating guilt, and discovered the nighest possible road to the regions of misery. All this may be considered as whimsical by the voluptuary and the infidel, but a blind man is no judge of colours. He knows not the difference between a pavement and a quagmire.

Another immutable and eternal principle is this, that it is humanity in any government to suppress books that teach men to make experiments, where the hope of success is not half so strong as the probability of miscarriage, and when irreparable misery must follow, whether their experiments succeed or prove abortive, after they are once attempted. Let us suppose that twenty or thirty thousand men, in a particular country, conceive and attempt to execute the plan of a revolution. If we could admit the possibility of their success, must we therefore infer that they would have changed for the better? If they got rid of an absolute monarchy for a democratical government, I conceive they only changed one tyrant for a thousand. But what right had they to come upon the nation by surprise, throw all into confusion, and thus involve the innocent, perhaps a thousand times more numerous than themselves, in all the wretchedness of a civil war? Let Mr Paine's principle be admitted, that what a nation wills to do, it has a right to do; yet from what source does one man out of a thousand derive his right to overturn an existing government; It would puzzle a wise head to give me an answer; and I here pledge myself to prove, that no revolution almost,

ever happened in any country with a much
larger proportion on its side. It began with
the knowledge of a few, and the majority stood
astonished at the unexpected explosion. They
might grumble and retreat from the scene of
action, but a public avowal of their discontent
would have conducted them to the scaffold.
Let the weather-cock determinations, the deli-
berate murders, the weekly constitutions, and
the indiscriminate butchery of guilt and innocence, speak aloud the frightful nature of all
popular governments. But suppose they
should fail of accomplishing their object, the
consequences are too obvious to require point-
ing out. They must fall the unpitied victims
of their own folly and extravagance.

Now, if a majority of perhaps two-thirds of
a nation are satisfied with their political constitution, the man who publishes, with a view
to disaffect them, is worthy of punishment,
and his works of being consigned to perpetual

oblivion. If they are not satisfied, I mean a great majority, it is their duty to express it in the form of a petition. Thousands have requested a reform in the representation of this country, but none, I believe, ever went so far as to demand a republic. Yet this would have been no more criminal than the writings of Mr R———s, who ventured to mention the lopping off two thirds of our excellent constitution, (the two houses of parliament.) The one was fully as much high treason as the other, and as repugnant to the nature of our constitution, as an Executive Directory would be, or a Council of Five Hundred.

It cannot be said that the power of restricting the press can be lodged any where so properly as in the hands of government, because if that restriction be intended to prevent the introduction and spread of impiety, anarchy and wickedness, government is only executing its deed of trust by every such interference. The absolute necessity of some restraint, by which its present licentiousness may be curbed, will admit of no dispute; but who, it may be said, are to determine its limits? When I say that every publication tending to increase useful knowledge, and to promote the interests of piety and virtue, is deserving of encouragement and public sanction, and that every work, however ingenious, which destroys rational liberty, moral obligation, and a love of what is excellent, ought to perish in manuscript, I apprehend that the limits are obvious to every understanding, and may be settled with the greatest ease. I humbly apprehend that to specify the nature of such productions as may be legally published, always keeping in view the increase of useful knowledge and moral improvement, would be a more eligible and less injurious method, than to require of every printer an enormous bond. My reason for thinking so is this. When the topics for discussion are stated in general terms, without condescending

on every particular, men are explicitly made
acquainted with the extent of their authority,
and rendered incapable of pleading ignorance
as an excuse. But it is conceiveable, that
many whose presses never groaned with blas-
phemy or sedition, who never printed any
thing unbecoming the dignity of human nature,
and the good order of society, may not be
able to give a bond for a thousand or two
thousand pounds. Men of considerable credit
and respectability in the world can seldom
procure sureties for such an immense sum.
Hence they must be excluded from employment, though they should be the only men of
the profession who deserve to be encouraged.
If the nature and extent of the subjects are
clearly specified, a bond, in my judgment, is
wholly superfluous, because every man must
be responsible for his violation of the law.
In the case of a bond, the people may suffer
who alone are innocent, while the man is ex-
emptedwho deserves to be punished. I should
consider this, not as any curb to the licenti-

ousness of the press, but a direct attempt to ruin the honest tradesman. It does not strike at the root of the evil, while it injures the art of printing as a commendable employment. It must be heavy, could it remedy the evil which it is intended to correct; and yet in proportion to its weight it would encourage monopoly, which is pregnant with mischief to every occupation. After specifying the nature of the subjects to be prohibited, let each transgression of the law be considered as seditious, libellous, or a misdemeanor, to each of which its proper punishment is already annexed by the jurisprudence of this country. Let author and printer be deemed equally criminal, and let nothing anonymous be given to the world. These or such like regulations will answer all the important purposes for which a restraint can be adopted, and prevent the many mischiefs that we presume must result from insisting on a bond.

But here I anticipate an objection which will no doubt be made against me, that all restraints of the forementioned kind, are outrages on that sacred and unalienable right—the right of private judgment. It is no doubt true, that none but the Almighty is privy to our secret thoughts, and that nothing short of omnipotence can controul our opinions. The right, therefore, of private or individual judgment is a pure nonentity, or at best altogether insignificant, if its operation must be confined within us, and if it may not be made manifest by words or writing. This would be the private judgment of a beast, if you will pardon the expression, to which nature has denied the faculty of speech. The deductions of reason from particular premises, and the coincidence or incongruity we may discover between ideas by means of comparison, would constitute a load of wretchedness instead of satisfaction, were an unconditional embargo laid on the faculty of communication which God has given us. Thus would the objector

no doubt reason, and so far he would reason
with propriety. But while it is impossible
not to venerate the right of private judgment,
I presume that no man can deliberately look
at the terrific consequences which have teem-
ed from the abuse of it in every age, without being alarmed. The right of private
judgment, like every other which nature has
conferred, becomes forfeited to society, the
instant it disturbs the public peace, because it
will ever be dangerous in proportion to its
power. Armed with the authority of the civil
magistrate, and impatient of restraint or oppo-
position, it has often deluged the earth with
innocent blood, and arrogated to itself the ex-
clusive privilege of dictating to others. Men
who thus think and thus act, may be deprived
of authority while their inclinations continue, so that we cannot ascribe any apparent
change to a renunciation of their former creed.
The lion may cease to devour when he is
chained, but in such a case we must ascribe
his conduct to his fetters, not to his disposition.

A man may deem it persecution to put the smallest restraint on his private judgment, but his opinion alters not the nature of things, which must be immutable and eternal. When that restraint is designed to prevent him from accumulating guilt, and bringing mischief upon others, it is certainly a favor, let him call it what he pleases. The abstract essence of things cannot be altered by vowels and consonants. If I may quote from that antiquated book, the Bible, we understand that Saul of Tarsus thought he should do many things contrary to the name of Christ, and therefore under such a persuasion he would have deemed it persecution to stop him on his way to Damascus, and confine him in prison. Yet he was afterwards fully convinced of the contrary; but it would not have altered the case although he never had.

I trust I shall live and die in the persuasion of this truth, that God never gave human nature a right, the immediate tendency of the exercise of which was to subvert the good order of society, and raise man in arms against man. The essential difference between a state of nature and of civilized life is this; that, in the former, every man is obliged to defend his person and property by individual exertion, whereas he throws in his rights into the other as into a bank, and draws upon the constitution for a redress of grievances. He is no longer his own judge or avenger, because such acts would imply the personal possession of those very rights which his claim to a connection with society point blank denies. I grant, indeed, that the rights given up to the guardianship and management of society, are such as are imperfect in the individual, which, it may be said, the right of private judgment is not. But it is equally true, that every right of which mankind can boast is subject to the controul of society, in so far as the exercise of them would disturb the general happiness. For instance, when a man inculcates opinions upon others, by all the artifice and sophistry

of which he is master, the manifest tendency
whereof is, to diminish our love of God and
our neighbour, and set open the flood-gates
of debauchery and injustice, he is as deserving of confinement as the midnight plunderer.
Society could not long exist without sacrificing
a lesser evil to a greater good, when necessity
requires it. If she did not thus act, she
would betray her trust, defeat the ends of her
institution, and cherish in her bosom the seeds
of her own destruction.

If there be any right perfect in the individual, it must be the one under consideration,
yet it would be barbarous in society never to
limit its exercise. We have seen already
what use the devotees of Rome have made of
it when unrestrained. Upon the same principle that a man looks up to the community
for a redress of grievances, which he could
not always do himself by corporeal punishment, though he were allowed, he must also
be persuaded that society is not bound to
defend his person and avenge his quarrel, and

yet allow him to do more mischief to thousands of her members than he could ever experience as an individual. But is not this doctrine, it will perhaps be said, founded upon the Roman Catholic persuasion, that persecution for conscience sake is highly meritorious? It is not. They who persecute for this reason, wish to step in between God and man, and dare the Almighty at his peril to receive the worship of his creatures. They profess uncommon zeal for the honor of Jehovah, and yet it is impossible to take a more effectual method of bringing him into contempt. What for a bloody monster is your God, may the persecuted say, when he requires us to barter our reason for a bundle of absurdities, and demands our lives if we refuse to comply? They who are persecuted cannot act so to others without renouncing their principles, while they who persecute cannot act otherwise, so long as they believe them. Such persecution is a premium for acts of wickedness, if the persecuted shall retreat through fear, and

a method which never made a steady convert
in the memory of man. But the doctrine of
this lecture dreams not of stepping in between
God and man, but between firebrands and
society in civil matters, to prevent that
mischief which individuals may do to thousands, and which in fact they would ultimately feel as well as others, if permitted
to continue. The man, therefore, who can
perceive no difference between this and persecution for conscience sake in religious matters, must be a more acute logician than Ari-
stotle himself. The restraints proposed in this
discourse, and which are deduced from eternal
principles, would indeed exclude many thousands of volumes from deluging the earth;
but they are such restraints as keep from man
no gratification to a refined taste, no useful
invention to the mechanic, no solid food for
an enlarged understanding, nor any real a-
musement which can be of service to our
nature. All the rest are like daggers in the
hands of a madman, or poison in the spoon of

a child;—sudden interference can alone avert the danger, which, when it proceeds a certain length, sets all remedy at defiance.

Those who pretend to develope the plans of government, and who ascribe designs to administration which it never publicly avowed, say, that the regulations concerning the press which have taken place since this Essay was composed, have no other view than to suppress every political performance of a republican tendency.* It is commonly observed, and with great judgment, that we are never to ascribe a man's conduct to unworthy motives, if we can find those which are commendable. Would it not then be more charitable to conclude, that the object of administration is to check the triumphant spread of impiety and wickedness, by attaching responsibility to the author of every licentious performance?

---

* It is equally the duty of government to suppress books of this, as well as any other description, provided their obvious effect is the wretchedness of the subjects.

The B——p of D——m made a motion some
time ago, respecting the more punctual obser-
vance of the Lord's day, and although it was
afterwards set aside without passing into a law;
who can tell but the present restraint on the
press may ultimately be productive of the
same salutary effects? I will venture to predict
that it must be so, though the present genera-
tion should not live to see it, since the most
rampant wickedness to which men have formerly had an unlimited access, will, in time,
be beheld in perspective. The fuel which
now feeds the fire of human depravity will be
gradually removed; and I hope it will not be
deemed extravagant to assert, that a new nation shall arise from the ruins of the old.

The liberty of the press was deeply lamented
by a noble real on his death-bed, because it
had given him the opportunity of disgracing
his character and wounding his conscience, by
the most infamous and villainous publication
with which the press ever groaned. If I may

depend on my information, he called in some
hundred copies at about £.5 each, to be committed to the flames.* This was after he
came to himself, for the greater part of his
short life was a state of insanity, worse than
ordinary madness. O, glorious liberty, which
makes a man tremble at himself when on the
verge of an eternal world, and willing to give
the universe, did he possess it, could he ob-
literate his extravagance for ever! Voltaire's
Philosophical Dictionary was burnt at Paris
by the hands of the common executioner,
in the year 1766, and it is pleasing to behold something of a similar spirit kindling up
in Britain.

* It will not perhaps be deemed impertinent to give the reader in
this place, a short anecdote of a sister of the earl's mentioned above.
She was a lady of consummate abilities, both natural and acquired,
but whose mind had been desperately corrupted by the liberty of the
press. Some gentlemen or noblemen taking occasion to praise her
brother in very handsome terms;——yes, said she, he would have
been a very clever man, had it not been for that old foolish thing
called *repentance!* Such language is terrible in the mouth of any
rational being, but it is monstrous beyond description in the mouth
of a female.

By the licentiousness which the press formerly enjoyed, it was possible for unprincipled men to assassinate their fellow creatures in the dark, without the danger of being brought to punishment. He who was, or thought himself injured by another, had it in his power to hold him up to the ridicule or contempt of the world, while the supposed culprit had not the opportunity of vindicating his character, or of taking vengeance on the cowardly assailant. If I am stopped upon the highway by a foot-pad, I may endeavour to save myself by running him through the body; but the rascal who attacks me in ambush from behind the liberty of the press, puts it out of my power to obtain satisfaction. While we cannot read the letters of Junius without admiring the poignancy of his wit, and considering the elegance and nervousness of his diction as wholly unrivalled by any writer, one is tempted at the same time to conclude, that all he says cannot be strictly true. If it is, why

did not Junius come forward in *propria per-
sona* ? Nobody can tell who Junius is, and
therefore while he lies hid behind the curtain
of a fictitious appellation, we can neither tell
who in reality we are to praise, nor who is
liable to feel the consequences of defamation,
if he has departed from veracity. To feast
in secret on the applause of mankind, is a
singular pitch of self-denial, and to be afraid
of danger, if convinced we have done our
duty, is the most contemptible weakness. No
man should be ashamed to avow the truth,—
a conduct proportionably meritorious as the
danger of doing it increases. But might not
Junius have been prosecuted, imprisoned, or
perhaps put to death, had he told his real
name ? I answer, let him die a martyr for the
truth, or for ever hold his tongue. If we may
meddle with things sacred in a political Essay,
why did not the Apostles act as Junius has
done ? Because they were convinced of the
infinite importance of the truths they delivered,

they gloried in being the publishers of them, and smiled at the arm of authority when lifted up to destroy them.

I consider every anonymous writer in the light of *Lingo* in the *Agreeable Surprize*, who, when out of the reach of danger, exclaimed with the magnanimous voice of a hero; " *fire away my brave Bellona !*" The man who puts not his name to his own performances, is either afraid or ashamed. If afraid, he must be conscious that he is not speaking truth, or if he is, I pronounce him an advocate that will do it more harm than good. If he is ashamed, his productions must be impious or profane, and as such, ought to be *damn'd* from the press.*

* This is not to be considered in the light of swearing, and there-fore it may be necessary to inform the unlearned reader, that when books are said to be *damned*, critics mean by it that they are consigned to oblivion. They are like ephemerons in the republic of letters; they are born in the morning, and perish at night.

A man has no reason to be ashamed of what is intended for the good of his fellow creatures, whether it be theology, philosophy, or any of the sciences. What he publishes may be weak, destitute of the graces of fine composition, and the masterly arguments of deep research; but if it is countenanced by the Almighty, and the monitor within, its author need not redden as if guilty of a crime. Nothing is shameful but what is criminal. Nor has he reason to be afraid when standing forth the advocate of injured truth and justice, since the worst that can happen him in so glorious a cause, ought to be a source of triumph. But may not the arm of power be sometimes disposed to crush the defender of truth, and hang or transport the man who appears its vindicator? If this should ever happen, the sufferer cannot bear a more honorable testimony for it, than by becoming an exile from his native country, or by the forfeiture of his life. But life is sweet, and a

man's native country has ten thousand charms.
Be it so, the restrictions imposed on the former licentiousness of the press, do not oblige
a man to defend the truth, but leave him the
alternative of silence, and the enjoyment of
his sentiments as an individual. If he will
write—if he cannot help shewing his talents—
if incurably smitten with the *rabies scribendi*,
it is surely reasonable that he should father
his own productions. If I rightly understand
the late regulations, they do nothing more than
oblige every author to avow his own performances, and certainly it is impossible to prove
that this is a restraint. If they punish, in one
shape or other, the authors of such publications as would formerly have passed with im-
punity, it must be proved that such punishment
is tyranny, and that the former negligence was
highly commendable, before it can be admitted
that such a measure is unjust. I could easily
prove it rational, political, benevolent and

wise, which I trust the present Essay will in some degree evince.

Men are accustomed to view the present subject through a *camera obscura,* if I may so express myself, which shews every thing in an inverted position. If we consider books, merely as the repositories of the opinions of mankind, without once adverting to their nature and probable tendency, it will indeed be difficult, if not impossible to prove, that the liberty of the press ought in any case to be circumscribed. But let pernicious principles, with all their fair and obvious consequences, take possession of the minds and deportment of the human race, and the whole enchantment is presently dissolved. I may keep a dagger, a musket, or a battering-ram in my cabinet of curiosities, but the instant I employ them against the life of a fellow creature, I become deserving of punishment. When I hear of a robber, a murderer, or one guilty of high.

treason, going to the gibbit, I dare not say that
he is cruelly treated; yet many licentious authors have done more permanent mischief to
immortal beings, than all the murderers upon
earth.

But why impose any restraints on the press,
when the sentiments of mankind ought to be
free as the air? I have as good a right as you
have, to deliver my opinion upon any subject
whatever, the very existence of which right is
denied, if I am to be punished for divulging
it. Have you not granted already, that printing is an admirable, a valuable invention, and
that to it we are indebted for our emancipation
from ignorance, and for that high degree of
intellectual improvement for which all men
either are, or may now be distinguished? This,
I apprehend, is the gordian knot of the whole
controversy, which, however, it will not be
difficult to undo. " Why impose any restraints on the press?" I answer, why impose
any restraints upon the thief, the robber, or

the murderer? The reasons which would be deemed conclusive in the one case, are a thousand times more so in the other. " He who steals my purse, steals trash."*—he who murders me, from whatever motives, cannot kill my soul; but the licentious author may so artfully infuse his poison, and by such imperceptible degrees, that I may be everlastingly ruined before I am aware. " I have as good " a right as you have, to publish my opinion " upon any subject whatever." That I most readily grant. This right we both received from the Almighty, and while our opinions continue in the abstract, or wholly detached from any thing but ourselves;—while we keep them in our minds, and communicate them to none, they are capable of being controuled by no being in the universe, the Almighty alone excepted. But the moment we divulge them, —as soon as we labour to make them be be-

* Shakespeare.

lieved, and adopted as principles of action, society has an indubitable right to judge whether they are pernicious or profitable, and to reward or punish in proportion to our deserts. The remaining part of the objection is therefore downright sophistry;—that the existence of the right is called in question, when our opinions subject us to punishment. It is not our opinions, considered purely as such, that render us liable to be punished. It is the effect we intend them to produce, and the industry we employ to propagate and enforce them, which constitute our guilt. For instance, were a man to say, " it is my humble " opinion that this country would be better " governed by a republic, but I may be " wrong, and therefore I offer it with the " greatest diffidence;" he could not be deemed punishable. But should the same man tell us—" I assert that the constitution of this " country ought to be republican, and nothing " shall be wanting on my part to convince the " people of its truth, and spur them on to

" obtain it;" let common honesty determine
if the case would not be radically changed.
By the former hypothesis his opinion is delivered with modesty; it is the language of a
man who requests information, and cannot be
productive of any dangerous effects. By the
latter, he avows himself the enemy of his
country, and resolves to bring ruin on the
whole community. I have a right to vindicate my innocence when unjustly accused, but
should I be found guilty of a capital crime by
a jury of my countrymen, would any person
be so absurd as maintain that this took away
my right to vindicate my innocence? Dread-
ful! No! I took it away in this case myself,
and freely forfeited my right to defend any
longer what I did not possess.

In fine, let the voluptuary suppose for a
moment that he has no beastly appetites to
please, the ambitious man no extravagant pro-
jects to execute, and the incendiary no infernal
thirst for tumult to satisfy, and I desire no

more. If such men make such suppositions, they will be astonished why they did not long since discover the very doctrine here defended, instead of censuring its author as an enemy to freedom.

POSTSCRIPT.

THE foregoing Essay was composed long before any restrictions on the press were agitated, either in the English or Irish House of Commons, except the late additional duty of two-pence on each newspaper may be viewed in that light. I believe that the members who brought in the bills, suggested the idea of insisting on a bond from every printer, but we are happy to understand that it has been finally relinquished. What I have said on the insufficiency of bonds as a radical cure for the evils complained of, seems to me to be founded on the nature and reason of things; it was not dictated by a spirit of opposition, and I can venture to call it the effusions of an honest heart. It is to me peculiarly gratifying, that the measures of government respecting the press appear to have my very reasoning for their basis, although my Essay was composed before their adoption. I have

always thought that the press required to be
restricted, ever since I was capable of reason
ing on any subject, and the more minutely I
examine the incalculable evils which its licentiousness has occasioned, the more deeply am
I persuaded that I have not been deceived.

It has been the means of shedding more innocent blood in a neighbouring country, than
ever was spilt by all the despots upon earth in
the same space of time. The people of France
have got rid of a despotic government; but
can human wisdom discover no medium between the horrid magnificence of absolute monarchy, and the fluctuating, unprincipled bawl-
ing of a democracy or a republic? The cry of
the multitude is, *Danton* to-day, and *Brissot*
to-morrow. In all popular governments there
is always a silly, unmeaning competition for
fame, and envy and jealousy distract and divide
them. The *Robespierre* of to-day becomes
the victim of to-morrow, and the transition
from the tribune to the guillotine is easy and

natural. Men will always be men, and when
the rabble are in authority, the consequence
will be a mob. When the whole mass have
the power of representation, there is no security
that wise and good men will be elected, for a
blind man, it is well observed, is no judge of
colours. The horrid massacres which have dis-
graced a neighbouring country, have originated
from the very texture of its political constitution. A *Custine* is chosen a general to command
a formidable army, and he glories in transmit-
ting accounts of his wonderful success. He
sometimes fails to carry off the palm of victory,
and yet in the midst of discomfiture he hopes
afterwards to be triumphant. But is *Custine*
dead? Yes. Did he then resign his breath in
the field of battle? No: envy and jealousy
found means to defame him, and the impetu-
osity of his zeal was rewarded with the guillotine. The antipathies and attachments of the
multitude are altogether unaccountable, and
when they have authority, they will accuse to
shew it. And from the accusation of the innocent, the transition is easy to the swearing to his

guilt. Myriads rejoiced at the murder of *Ma-rat*, and the Convention punished the perpetrator of the deed. But behold the stock-jobbing nature of public opinion where there is no settled authority. The remains of *Ma-rat* are interred with honor, and they are afterwards dug out of the earth to be branded with disgrace! When the question is put, Could a *Custine*, a *Robespierre*, a *Danton*, a *Brissot*, and a thousand other victims of popular fury, be all guilty of capital crimes? Charity recoils with horror, and even stern justice hangs down her head and blushes. But when men are once countenanced in defamation, they convert it into a trade, and live upon its emoluments. In all popular governments, the man whose conduct is at one time inserted in the bulletin, may be denounced at another as an enemy to his country, without any cause, and at last finish his career upon a scaffold. Who is that great, pacific, and beloved personage, on his way from Swisserland to Paris? It is the illustrious *Barthelemy*. He comes to the metropolis incognito, that his chariot may not be drawn along by an applauding populace. But in an instant, before he has time to let either France or any other country feel the salutary effects of his uncommon abilities, he is arrested and sentenced to banishment, without even the formality of a trial. If he had accusers, they were kept behind the scene, and neither witnesses nor jury were summoned to do him justice. I believe all Europe rejoiced when *Robespierre* was guillotined, but what if France should prove a hot-bed for rearing such monsters? Nay I venture to predict, that it will never want *Robespierres* so long as it is a republic. All these blessed consequences have originated from the liberty of the press. But objects at a distance affect only the intelligent few, while the multitude are touched with those alone which they feel to be calamitous. Let us therefore come nearer home, and see what has been done among ourselves by the liberty of the press. The enlightened part of the community, I believe, had no other object in

view by all their clubs and petitions, than a
reform in Parliament; but there were, and
still are countless thousands among us who
look a great way beyond this. I do sincerely
believe that the measures of government have
been intended to prevent us from plunging
into the gulph of a revolution. This, I
honestly confess, was not always my opinion,
for I viewed the treason and convention bills,
the suspension of the Habeas Corpus, and
such like measures, in a very different light.
But I must now acknowledge that all these
regulations have been the result of dire necessity, when I look at the present miserable state
of Ireland. But perhaps it will be said that
its pitiable condition is the effect, not the cause,
of such regulations. I deny the assertion.
If we consider the magnitude of this rebellion,
and the uncommon caution with which it has
been conducted—if we advert to the time absolutely necessary to ascertain the genuine sentiments of eighty or a hundred thousand men,
together with their oaths of allegiance to be

true to their trust, and the unexampled manner in which they accumulated weapons, by
conducting them to the grave like deceased
friends ;—it will be impossible not to see, that
it had been projected before the commencement of the war with France, when none of
the regulations complained of had any existence. If it was then seen by Mr Pitt, when
only in embryo (a supposition neither extravagant nor improbable,) it follows that the war
with France furnished him with an opportunity of raising such a formidable army as
might be sufficient to check that rebellion in an
instant, whenever it should openly appear.
To have said, six years ago, that such a rebellion would have existed in Ireland, would not
have been believed neither in nor out of the
House of Commons. The Minister might of
consequence have been prevented from guard-
ing against the evil, till the disease had grown
too desperate for any remedy to subdue.

Who are the rebels in Ireland, and for what are they contending? I need not say who they are, nor that their object is the final overthrow of the British constitution, let them ascribe their conduct to whatever they please. It is similar to the desperate attempts of the Pretender, in the years 1715 and 1745, and therefore to bewail the situation into which they have plunged themselves, is to lament that we are not hanged, drowned, and burnt, for the sake of conscience! It is a pity that the public at large do not understand their principles, for then the conduct of administration towards Ireland would appear in a very different light from what it does to many. In one word, if the Irish insurgents are what we all know them to be, the man who can condemn the vigorous measures of Government, after such hostile and formidable preparations, might as well honestly tell us that he is sorry he cannot see something like the Irish massacre, the year 45, or the revocation of the Edict of Nantz.

B.

If it be as manifest as the equality of two and two to four, that all the evils formerly mentioned, and a thousand others which intended brevity allowed us not to consider, have originated from the press, it will strike every rational being that it has had too much liberty. Many will consider the smallest restraint as tyranny at first, but as soon as mankind come to themselves, the scene will be changed. The universal exclamation will then be,—what fools have we been to court our own destruction, to admire only such books as set us together by the ears, eradicated every principle of moral obligation, and made us run stark mad in pursuit of butterflies! God be praised for a return of reason, which we will never prostitute in time to come, as alas, we have done in days that are past!

F I N I S.

W. HALLGARTH, JUN. PRINTER;
SOUTH. SHIELDS.

www.ingramcontent.com/pod-product-compliance
Lightning Source LLC
Chambersburg PA
CBHW031756090426
42739CB00008B/1037